Easy & Concise Guide for Contentment and Sustained Happiness

KADAMBARI MADHOK

ISBN: 9798525030442

DEDICATION

This book is dedicated to the supreme love of nature which it ushers on us, so
relentlessly!
This book came into existence due to my father and was possible to write, with
the beautiful and undying support of my lovely husband and children.

CONTENTS

ACKNOWLEDGMENTS

I am truly grateful to all the people whom, I have ever known. Their wisdom and the experiences I had with them, have made me who I am today and which in turn have contributed to the richness of this book. Special thanks to my father Ashok Bhasin and mother Sudha Bhasin for giving me, all that can be given!

Chapter 1

Introduction – The Energy

What should the aim, of this book be? Popularity of book/author - no, popularity of concepts - no (as concepts keep changing, everybody's boat is different, different concept fit differently, truth that we all seek, is multi- faceted in each situation, at different times). You are free to improvise by adding your own ideas, as your own truth will be unique to you. And your own concepts, will fit in differently to your very own situations. Reading this book, should reveal your very own truth to you - at any given place, time, circumstances unbound by any of these elements.

Energy flows in everything, right from the electrons running through the wire - to bring light in front of you right now! To your fingers holding the book to read and mine to write. This energy, which is revered by Albert Einstein in his equation, E=mc2; Hawking in his black hole theory; Bohr's in his Copenhagen statement/entanglement theory; Bell in his theorem trying to explore quantum physics; Cosmologist in their theories, is the most intriguing element that exists.

It flows so freely, in the currents of rivers, in oozing lava, geysers, budding and saplings. Some of it, is stored as potential energy like in mountains, in Earth's crust while other is dynamic and explosive in nature. Mysteriously in the womb, we grow from a cell to a whole person. If you stop thinking everything else and just give it a thought, to this energy that is so pure, and which gives life to us in this amazing way!

Connection to Laws of Energy - *Revelation prologue*

As we know the *law of conservation of energy* follows the rule-energy can neither be created nor destroyed, it just changes form from one to another. It keeps changing. Be it, of the light to the form of heat, deer to the form of lion, bones to the form of dust, soil to the form of plant seed, plant seed to the oil, to the energy dispensed to this finger permitting me to write this now and present it to you. While you are holding the book or device in your hand to read it. But, yet it remains the same.

Second law of thermodynamics states, that energy moves from high pressure to low pressure, meaning energy is always trying to establish an equilibrium. Be it the global weather, evaporation of sweat from your hands, or homeostatic equilibrium which every cell of your body, with every change in your body's environment, constituents etc., is trying to achieve every second of the hand clock, even right now as you read.

In this complicated chaotic system of ever-changing forms of energy, always trying to reach somewhere/some state/some point. We creatures too, paint a similar picture. Always running after situations/person, so that we can be content in some or the other way. But where is that point, this state which is the ultimate? We have to find it somehow, in anytime. The sooner, the better for us, and for the connections of the energy.

Newton's law of universal gravitation states that every particle attracts every other particle with a force, this force (F) can be represented by this equation F= $\underline{G\ m1m2}$

$$r^2$$

where G is the gravitational constant, m1 and m2 are the masses of the two objects and r is the distance between the centers of the objects.

Hence, we can infer that every particle visible to eyes or even minute particles nonvisible to eyes like quark, gamma rays, X-rays etc have some influence over each other, through some force.

We simply cannot deny, a larger force at work which is influencing things visible and non- visible affecting our reality- of day to day lives. And this can be calculated too!

Main point is, we all are connected in some ways - on some levels. How much precisely, to which minute levels? Scientists over decades have been working on this question and are still working on it.

Be it quantum physics or Astro physics, nobody has been able to solve the full comprehensive workings of energy, the driving force of a quark or something smaller than quarks. And this is endless, as you go deep into the entanglement theory or Copenhagen interpretation the particle behaviour does not make sense. Hence, you cannot comprehend everything with mind alone, you need your heart, soul/ those inner eyes to comprehend it all. We all share a space outside; we know, we do- on Earth. But we do that within as well, which is somehow connected to this enormous, mysterious source of energy.

But the key, to this vast, infinite, mothering or destroying – Energy or you can even say the source of happiness and contentment, lies within us and which is said, by various religious texts/gospels, over millennia of years.

Inspection

So, what is the key? How to get it?

We all are the same from within, they say.

Let us inspect this further.

1) We taste the same thing as same- food would taste same to me as to you, saltless food will taste the same saltless, to me as to you. Sweetness will taste as sweet to you, as to me.

2) If I burn my hand by accident, I will have the same sensations as you.

3)   Now more subtle, If I see a crippled baby trying to walk, I will feel the same pity for him/her as you would.

Hence, if we see scientifically the variables keeps changing, that is us - as in essence, but the constants above remain the same. Somethings do not change. Therefore, there is something unchangeable within us. Hence, we all are same, from the inside core.

Therefore, if I say I have the key, so it can be yours too. Because I am not any different from you. Same species, same ever-changing world.

Chapter 2

The Introspection - Your Task

- Not, to get stuck in the nitty gritty of things, like which language I have used? How have I presented? Which finger is used, to point to the revelation? Who the finger belongs to? Why is a finger used? Rather than this, concentrate on what is been revealed. Be a real scientist, sticking to the path, to find out the main aim of the qualitative scientific pursuit. Which is finding out the truth, only the truth, and nothing but the truth. Not getting stuck anywhere else, not in apparatus, methods/ ways used by you, leading to, your very own truth, revealed to you- by you.

❖ Do not revere the revelation. It is very simple to attain, and common to everybody. Do not, put it on a pedestal so high, that it seems unreachable to you and only dust mites reach them and devour them. As discussed, we all are same, it can be even you in fact, writing this book, we are so similar!

After all, we all are one, which is even scientifically proved. As I listened to, a National Space Centre Planetarium, introduction speech, snuggled with my kids, it echoed the age-old science, mixed with spirituality. The lady who led the talk introduced us to the topic, "We are all stardust" meaning we have been recycled again and again, from gas and dust particles of a star- to a planet- to different species over different centuries and now we are, what we are today. This resounds, with the theory of energy changing one form to another. Hence, we all are one indeed, recycled again and again. Irrespective of what intellectual, emotional, or spiritual level we are at. In the end, we all are similar, coming from and going to the same source.

Because always we tend to revere- the things that are not ours- the people and situation which belong to us, at any given present moment, are of less value to us, in any section of life taken. We are constantly running for, and after situations, that we think might, bring contentment. Believe me, in fact, what you have right now, are the most precious people and situations that you might ever possess (good loving people support you, negative people teach you, how not to end up, like them, or some other valuable lesson to you) this is true for any   given time. And you can start this pursuit of self-discovery anytime, as it is simply not bound to time, any objects, situations, person, or a group. The only thing that matters is you, and your life and how you can achieve your own truth, if you set, your heart to it.

❖ Be always true, at least to yourself, keep the eyes of your soul, always open. The first thing to do, is to relieve yourself of any situation in past that might produce any hint of guilt within you, for in the present moments- correct it right away! Apologise, set things right. Because then only, you will be able to love yourself, which is the first step leading to your- magnanimous self. We can always see ourselves better in a clean mirror, rather than a stained mirror. And we do need a clear vision, to view and then take our journey from finite to infinite. Just like, only a mere grain of sand, can also reflect/encompass - and show sun in its view. Similarly, however small you consider yourself, in whatever sense, you still have the capability of seeing the sun or shining like the sun/ the source within. If ever so, you think you might be in, some situation, that you are unable to bring the change, and take away that guilt, then do not worry as long as you have clean conscience, that is all is needed. It is never too late, start doing things the right way, so that nothing makes you smaller in your own eyes.

❖ Be it anything that you do or things happening to be shaping your existence, always observe- just do not be oblivious to events. In present moments, you might lash out on somebody in anger, or get involved in something you feel guilty of later, do not judge yourself. Just, observe that you did it, or it happened through you, without being judgemental about the situation or to yourself. There are many innate desires with which, we are born with, and we sometimes get entangled in them and respond quickly to the situation, be it then anger, jealousy, comparison insecurity etc and we do it, without giving it a second thought.

Consider your situation at any given time as an event, where the control of the experiment is your reaction which is bound to happen while at any given time in your test (in scientific term) it is the introspection that matters. Introspection of the reaction of yourself, brought about by the situation. Experiment with it, letting it go or holding on to it, for truth-the ultimate goal. You have many options- hold on to it for self-pity/negative outcomes or merely, take it as an impression to gain insight about yourself, and/or as a tool to maybe, change in future, on how to deal with similar situations. Or simply let go for peace within self. Keep learning about your own self, in all the given situations. Remember you are the key. The more you know about yourself, the easier it is to work on self, to recognise patterns of behaviours and improve, if need be.

Believe in science, observe your own self and situations, make them as your materials/apparatus and as a true scientist, forever keeping the eye on the aim of the truth-about yourself, which is in turn linked to the universe.

But I must warn you, everything should be done smoothly, naturally. Without even a pulling a line on forehead, then only it will yield results. If it becomes heavy or tedious, you will be pulled down by the labour of it all.

I am still working on myself, and will do, till the end of my time. I believe as in my case, you shall reach a point where everything stabilises, as I said earlier you are the key. And with recognition of even a glimpse of true self, will be the end of all your qualms.

As we all know that the aim of any scientific experiment, is always to uplift or bring light to something, person in our case or the whole humanity. The desired result- of finding the aim of the ultimate truth- is to bring about true contentment, which is unphased by time/ situation posed on the self. Life is mysteriously beautiful just like science, and it keeps shedding petals of knowledge, to reveal a new core every time.

❖ Come may what, you can start at any given time, any situation, start observing yourself- start your journey. Do not be judgemental about yourself, you can always start over again, from fresh, and gain a new perspective of internal workings, regardless of the chaos of life around you, at this very present moment. Do not be afraid to make your own life rules, according to your own unique situation, your inner self will guide you, indicating what is right or no. Anything you do, which gives you no guilt of any sort. You are on the right path. After all, every religion says, God resides within you, so why not introspect this and get connected to ultimate reality, which will not leave you even when you die, as you would grasp the eternal chain!

❖ Rome was not built in a day they say!

One thing, I have learnt is- showing patience is particularly important- to each and every situation that is connected, with the want or need, you feel in life. Because life does not give you everything in a plate, that is for sure. First, even the Albatross chick must wait and strengthen his wings, to fly high in the sky like he/she owns it. So, it will take time to train your mind and getting into the habit of observing your own self. When life is going on, you will dip in and dip out of your own conscious pattern, but soon will get the hang of it. Remember, it takes lots of experiments to reach to a theory, your very own theory and then to establish the result- of the whole process. The whole purpose of which is enjoying the fruit of unphased spirit upliftment.

❖ Never doubt your inner self. Because if you, do it, you will be disconnected with almost everything. Self-doubt will also lead you to just seeing things negatively. In physics, a ball will keep on rolling until a force is applied to it, so your passion for self-pity or doubt, will keep on increasing until you apply brakes/ or smaller force than this a little bit of friction to begin with. This can be done, by acknowledging the fact that you are not alone, and we all are connected to something- that is higher than us. We can at least, have a glimpse of this higher self if we try! As you must have heard several times, we talk about gut feeling or follow your heart - this is true in any time given. As the thread that connects us all, shows us path everyday everyway, just we must be able to- listen to our own consciousness. You can see the suggestions or thoughts rising within you. It is your own call to sabotage them and go on living oblivious or listen to them and start on this amazing journey, to your own magnanimous self.

* Do not resist anything, unless its health threatening, or linked to mortality like drugs, smoking etc. So, in short no need to feel guilty or give up things that make you feel happy, as long as they are not harmful for your health or harm anyone else in the process. Just like, third law of motion states that each action has an equal and opposite reaction. The more you resist, the more of that urge will imprint your consciousness and it will cloud your thoughts up with this thing or habit, in a very subtle way. Thus, imprinting your thought process with something that is unnecessary or not needed at all. Making a clean/free consciousness difficult to attain. Because let us face it - we

live in a world where temptations, are bombarded at us from all angles. Instead, of excluding yourself of things, that you might think- will offer you purity of heart and soul, try to include and add more routines and rituals to your life. Meaning instead of contracting yourself, expand yourself and your consciousness. For example, you might follow a strict sugar free diet for 1 year, after a year of this resisting routine -there will come a moment where you might think about it, so much that you will succumb, to the urge and eat a bite or two. Thus, making you feel guilty unnecessarily. Now at the same time, if you start eating fruit whenever you feel the urge of eating sweet, that might do the trick. So instead of resisting the innate urges find your own way of tacking urges in a less aggressive way, so that you do not think about it all the time.

Many religion revere celibacies, I think it is simply going against nature. Being first of all a human, with all the urges experienced and tamed of- can only lead you to become your own supreme self. So, anything done in a natural way without hurting or causing trouble to others should be taken forward. These urges should be handled in such a way that you do not keep thinking about it all the time, it should be like a part of routine, like brushing teeth, do you think about brushing teeth all the time, fantasize it. You do not even, give it a thought. That is how, all urges should be calmed down, leading them to be less prominent so that they make less noise in your brain/thoughts. In this world, nothing is more harmful other than a clouded consciousness and how we think about things. If we are not obsessed by anything or any routine, that I would say that is nirvana, doing it but not affected by it. When you think about something, be it anything, you give it importance and cloud your thoughts or conscience with it, you do not let yourself be free of thoughts. Or in other words, you urge yourself to have a disbalanced thought process. Hence, do not give up on anything, do that particular thing or ritual till it is normal and not holding you down, do not take away but add things like love, respect for anyone and everyone. And believe me, if you are doing something truly wrong your inner self will reflect it as guilt, and you would instantly know, that it is wrong. As long as, you are not hurting anybody in anyway, including yourself you are fine.

❖ Most importantly all that I would write will just be words - until you start living them, feeling them!
Even more important is, to do things, that brings peace and joy to you (without the feeling of any guilt). These pathways may be completely different from what I say or point to, but in the end your true happiness- in the present moments is what matters and nothing else!

Not even the ultimate truth, can give you happiness until, it is not the truth of your life. And believe me, it is so simple to attain that you will be amazed.

When you kill the demons in your head, you are left with nothing else but peace. And this is, what is heaven, on Earth or nirvana or Jannat as people say. When you enjoy the smallest of pleasures in life, without getting entangled in them with -no stress, just float like a cloud casting a shadow on everything yet still remain, above everything.

Chapter 3

Human nature - The Revelation begins

❖ **Time as the element**

You have heard of it several times- be in the present moment.

Listened to it but taken no heed of it. You must- start it now, right this very moment.

Human nature is to think and remember specifically more negative things rather than positive. It likes to dwell on the past negatively, mull over things again and again.

We would not remember the 20 positive comments we got from a project, but we will hang on to one, negative comment and feel negative about it.

You have the key right now. Altogether stop thinking about awful past experiences, incidents and come back to the present moment.

It is like you are playing the record again and again of a song that does not exist in this time.

As you flap your wings too much against the different angles of time, you will sway from your landing. Flap your wings with time smoothly, with the angel of wind, and your landing will be smoother or perfect- **It starts with you**.

.

Key-

Initially you will have to train your mind. Tell a trusted person/companion - somebody close to you, that they remind you, every time that you go in past. They remind you, that you are going in the pit again. They keep doing it until you are set free.

Soon you will get the hang of it, you will be a free bird, a seed with endless potential, a roof without ceiling, the infinite self with no limitations.

Living in present moment is a key

❖ Ego as the element

Ego is a complex thing. You should know how to recognise it when it is playing up unnecessarily. How to use it wisely and when to let go of it. Also, when to hold on to it when it is necessary to do so.

Ego- gives you identity. After all you are nobody, without any identity. We take a form of a human and gain identity of an- entity by a name, nature etc. In essence, we get recognised by our name and character.

In this world of different physical forms, we must respect the forms.

For a simple example, it is essential for mother to have an ego, to protect her child from any probable harm coming to child. Which is pretty obvious, for example, if a cockroach crawls past the baby, or a lion comes close to baby. She should have the ego, of the mother form, and be ready to protect her child from the form of that creature. She cannot say that everything has the same energy, and I revere that energy, I will not do anything harmful to that creature. If she thinks like this - she will lose her child. At this moment, her ego is essential to save her child or herself from the harm. So, she needs the ego to protect her form in simple sense. Similarly, sometimes you have to protect yourselves from other people's behaviour, actions so they do not take you for granted. So, go ahead and protect yourself- your form, to make it stay healthy and hearty. Do not feel guilty while doing it. You are just protecting yourself, if you are too restless about something, that you did to protect yourself, just say sorry/pray internally to that person's energy and ask for forgiveness and that you had to take that step, to protect yourself. This way, the eyes of your consciousness are open, and you just see it is an incident resulting in protecting yourself which is the right, of every living being.

One, also should not carry their ego around. This task becomes very heavy and tedious with time. If you carry your ego around, I am intelligent, I am rich, I am talented, I am etc. You have to pay a price of the restlessness created by it, because there will be always someone more beautiful than you, clever than you, richer than you, unless you are the richest man on Earth- who wants to maintain his richest title (tedious for him/her as well) as everything has a price!

Go through this journey as a free form, just enough so that the ego can survive and protect itself from physical/mental harm or financial abuse, not an iota more than that. Because if you hold on to more than that, you falsely get trapped in a mirage, which makes you restless for more and more. More beauty, more money, more power, more fame, and it will never let you rest. You will keep running a race, with no sight of the end. Even the most powerful, almighty character of God, as seen in various religions does not have ultimate power, so that so, everyone thinks of him/her all the time. We forget him/her and carry on our errands and jobs oblivious to her/him. God is also not that powerful, that he/she gains attention of everybody at all times. As per different religions, he/she has also taken different forms and was bound by that form's life, obstacles/time in their paths and acted accordingly to the situations posed. So, I ask what is more to achieve in this life other than peace, contentment, and love for the self.

Just go through every moment of this life as a student, ready to learn-about yourself, about the sacred link you possess, that is connected to everything that exists. Although not with an ego, that I know everything and possess everything. I personally do not have full knowledge of how this complex web of perfection works – this energy works. Who claim to have - are lying? Because this knowledge's, full comprehension is beyond logic. But yes, I know my truth and am ready to share with you. I can show you the path taken, and you can find yours, along the way- as everything is connected. As it revealed to me, it will be revealed to you all by your very own self.

Key-

One is drawn to the attention to their own self, only when someone else is in front of themselves. For example, baby's consciousness just exists, and does not recognise itself, unless it is told it has got a name -an identity when compared with others. Same way ego comes into action when we compare. Do not look at anybody else's possessions, eye them and put them on your wish list. If it comes from within, then you really need it.

Get the difference between wanting and needing. Because when you compare yourselves with others, you get lost in the ego game. Realise this fact -there is no other, everybody is same from inside. If you want to become like them, become one from within, as you have potential to become and have everything possible in this universe. Rather than, asking for just some merely worldly objects (that are the cause of ego pumping- which always ultimately, leads to disappointment) blow up your ego, to the infinite level which includes everything and everybody. That way nobody else will exist, you will see yourself in everybody else. And everything and everyone will be one. One energy that circulates between all of us. Just like, you forgive yourself easily in some matters, you will have the strength to forgive other as well. If I can make mistake, so can they. You will let go of other people's behaviour towards you, as you know that are really made from the same matter, their emotional or intellectual projections might be different. But this is how, they will lose the power of hurting you.

My trick is, whenever someone hurts me knowingly/unknowingly I protect myself at the same time. I just say to myself, that they are drop of same energy which I love so much. Do their projections matter in the grand scheme? These people are bound by the instincts of the form/identity, they have taken in this life, I do not feel bad or negative then, and I move on in life without getting stuck.

Balancing ego is a key

❖ Love as the element

Everybody and everything, is bound by a pure emotion called love. We do everything and be it anything, we do, we do it because or out of love. Be it, love for a person/ a goal/ an idea, or an object. Love is the force that guides/ defines us and makes us do unimaginable things, on the path of our life. It makes us do these special feats unimaginable to our own eyes too, sometimes. It is seen even in the most inert, of the phases- like love for being lazy. It drives all our moves and actions- not only in long term goals but short term and even daily living too.

We just must be in love with ourselves to reach to the source. As all the religions and philosophies of the world, point to the inside core as the main source, which is connected to the main powerhouse of energy or the revered god. Hence, we should keep our conscience clean and then there will be nothing stopping you, from loving yourself. As the inside core of everybody, without any efforts given or taken is beautiful and pure. What is needed is removal of stains, from our own core's mirror of consciousness.

Being in love with somebody/something and being- true to it, in any given circumstances is crucial. Be it, you are in love with - an idea of your own god/ nature/ truth or a person. Because true love will always last, as it comes from within. There will be various obstacles in your path, ones that are unimaginable, even to the mere capabilities, of human being endurance. But if you stick to your love- be true to your love, your inner core will guide you through situations, telling you what is right or wrong? You just have to listen to it, endure all the blows that the time and situations present in front of you, and you shall have the flame burning still within you. Then that, is the real victory! Time and situations cannot take away your own positivity that is love = your source of happiness. Then, everything will be clearer, door will open to inner peace and contentment. Come may whatsoever, nobody or nothing can take your love away from you, and great thing you genuinely are in love with it, no efforts require for you there!

Key-

Love unconditionally till the end – Is the key

❖ Selflessness as an element

If you think about yourself all the time, you will end up being negative and miserable, at the end of every situation. Because, either you will feel, you are not getting what you want, or the situations/person are being unfair to you. If you take your focus from- not how much you receive, but how much you share. A journey form me to you or us, then things will start being different. Ask what can I do to make things better for the other person, or person around you, or the whole world? You should do this not for everybody else's sake, but for yourself, to take yourself away from self- pity. Because, even if you want to become the greatest person, or one form that has it all, in any given time- holding everything in one person's hand, is not possible. You have to lose yourself, your self to merge or become one with everything and everyone. One person cannot hold, everything positive in this world, or become the key. It is the uniform spread of energy that works. As energy is always trying to achieve, the law of energy equilibrium. The energy is spread from high energy to low, and then goes back to high. Similarly, one person cannot stay on the peak for long, as he or she has to come down in trough. Nobody can be ace in all of the aspects of their life, at all times. You can view it, in different celebrities and personalities lifestyle. They come- up from down, stay up for some time, and then suddenly, some part of their life gets affected, and they come spiraling down. Therefore, the key to contentment is leaving - I, behind and concentrate on us, and let (us) - take over. Us could be your family, your company for which you work, country you live/work for. As working or thinking of (I), will be limited but thinking or working for us is unlimited, and it has no definitions. Plus, you gain contentment, for achieving something that effects everybody, in a broader way, and uplifts everybody along with yourself.

Key-

Key is that you simply have to shift your focus, from me- to - you or us. Otherwise, things will not gain momentum. You will be stuck in your past impression and will feel like a victim all the times. You will feel you are bearing unfairness, about something, or you will constantly think, about any situations borne by you.

And as we all know, one does not stop learning, we must keep learning, till the end of our lives or sometimes, we are forced to learn. Even at the old age, one is forced to learn new ways of living adjusting to physical restrictions etc. Hence, now is the time simply to be new you!

Remember that you are losing every second of your precious life.

In this life, in which you could start new all over again. By getting stuck in some or the other way, you are robbing yourself from a potential of a new fresh start, which can start from, every second flying by in front of you, even right now, as you read!

Selflessness, giving up self-pity is another key.

Science and questioning as an element

Nobody is perfect, no one person, can be. People even found faults, with godly figures who took birth, long time ago. In any given situation, if you ask 100 people about a single statement you had made, some people will take your statement or situation positively while others negatively. People will react to whatever you do, or even, that you do not do sometimes. Because every inaction or action, we do have - implications. Each action has some reaction. After all, we live in a very complicated world, and that is for sure that, we cannot live as a hermit living high up in mountains. We have to survive in this ever-changing world. We are bound to be part of situations/things, thrown at us from different angles, all the time.

Be your own judge. Do not respond or pay heed to other people's reaction, but to solely your very own. How you see yourself, and what difference do you want in the situation. And, how to achieve it, should be your only goal. As they say, be your own competitor.

Key-

Do not stop questioning everything you see or hear? Even to what you read in this book. Become a true inquisitive being, and thus, thereby- you will start on your journey of self-discovery.

Start Questioning the truth as the key

❖ Self-competition or untouched by others is an element

Everyone has a different beginning of life, their own path, and the journey through life. We come across so many people, who are in their different phases of life. So please do not get intimidated by, how much somebody has, and you do not, or somebody has achieved and that you have not. As, they say there will always be people above and below you. And in any aspect considered, there will always be people better off than you, and many people worse than you. So why simply get distracted by these other people? Let them be on their path of peak and troughs, and you be on yours. As it is our eye, which always catches others peaks and gets jealous. This is natural I say, it can be seen very clearly and very much evident, even in toddler's behaviour patterns. But we have to rise above it and grow. That is what we are here for – Growth!

If we look closely, life has a rule, it will take away whatever you want and just give you whatever you need to grow. If you want a particular thing or situation, life will delay in giving it to you. The object or situation will be given to you at a time when you do not particularly desire it. Or you are enraptured in different angle of life, that the joy of the desired thing, does not hold much significance- at that present moment. As you would have moved on, from that desire or want. Even though, you might enjoy it for a while, soon it will not give you the joy, you thought it will give you. You become use to it. This holds true for any object or external thing, for example you wanted a Porsche - you worked hard for it (or let us say you did not), and you got it, at that particular time you felt joy and felt accomplished, but that joy does not last that long. Maybe it might last for a month. As you possess it, the feeling will become regular or mundane, you will look out for some other thing now. It ultimately failed to fulfil you with joy, that lasts for all the present moments and the future. Such are the ways, of the material things that can be possessed. While if you work and invest in building your own self, into such a refined being, that does not get affected by anything, that life or situations throws at you. But you are also happy and content, with anything or even nothing. Life should be about not be about contracting oneself but grow ourselves into something big and expansive. Be your very own competitor and challenge yourself into becoming bigger and bigger until no boundaries exist.

Key-

Key- Do not mull over other people's possessions and situations. The minute you start practising this, it will give you immense peace and contentment in whatever time or situation you are in life.

Not comparing with other people is the key

Chapter 4

The Revelation

As we look around calmly, we can see the beautiful scene of the rising sun, full moon in its glory, gurgling energetic river, lush green forest that remains forever like this. There is always plus and minus of species that exist, but forever these are - untamed, mysterious, serene, and calm, connecting us to something- that lies dormant within. When we see these natural scenes, they relax us and shows us that the connection that would last forever. Whatever life throws at us, or we are going through, the connection with nature, always remain the same whether we look at the sky as a 6-year-old, or at 60 years of age. It still amazes us, and shows us there is something higher than us, governing this world. We can call it energy, higher self, or God but we can say that something surreal, is there with us on our path, why not embrace it and make it a part of us, and also avail its energy in our daily living.

Everything has a lifespan, even our very own star-the sun. The scientists predict this that we all will dissolve, in something of a star or planets after its collapse. Is not this the proof enough that- we are connected in a major way- to the nature and amongst ourselves- to everything! So why not celebrate it, celebrate our eternity, which is even proven scientifically? so why not stop fretting about future or present situations? And start living like a king, every second of our lives!

Something in you does not change, you might get older with time, but you feel the same inside, people might recognise you differently- older, fatter, slimmer, etc. but you remain the same inside. This something - people call as soul, seer, spirit, atman etc. and that is the piece of energy, that is beyond the different experiences you have, considering even the time factor. This soul element can give you the insight to the main energy source of everything, to that ever existed, exists, and will ever exist. You just have to feel it, it is very subtle, and you can make its presence strong, by always listening to this inner voice, which is invariably correct each and every time

The quantum entanglement theory of quantum physics and quantum biology shows that every particle is linked to another particle in a mysterious way, and has some kind of power over another particle, through which they decide their whereabouts, and their descriptions in space, at any given time. Similarly, everything and every form is connected in the subtle zone of physics, biology, and psychology. If we see closely, when we do something, we can perceive in advance-what others might think of us, related to that particular topic. If we see clearly, how can you know their thoughts, unless we all are the same and are connected at some level?

Be it the quark, which formed a single cell of your muscle fiber-which is holding the book or the reading device that you are holding right now - to the atom of let us say Sun/ star or a planet. We all are interconnected. Physicists and astrophysicists are still trying to marry up, and provide a solid evidence to connect, the microscopic laws of physics that is quantum mechanics-to macroscopic laws of how planets and star move and behave like the theory of relativity.

We all are formed from the same natural elements and are same from inside.

As it is cited, that spacetime, is the fourth-dimension present.

According to interpretation of Copenhagen statement- by scientist Neil Bohr. There is something that changes or does not change, and that remains unobserved over the time, unless, observed by somebody. It comes into existence at the precise moment, of the observation, by the observer. Meaning it is all about the observation and the observer. If, you do not observe yourself or the universe or the energy. Things or events will keep on happening randomly (or with a pattern maybe). But, when you start observing your own journey, or your own self, through your very own inner eyes. A pattern emerges and you can then, try to reach some stability of some ideas, that, this is, what is life all about. Although, life can throw a curve ball, whenever it wants but still it will enable us to see, and know the patterns of peak and troughs of time, and situations etc. With the observation of the subtle, we will be close to the subtle, which is the silent essence of existence of everything and every being. Hence being an observer is an important thing in this journey. Big things or events brings limited joy, it is the subtle things that brings the joy to you. Which makes you feel light and expansive, like- a smile from your child; that moment when you see love in your partners eyes, these subtle moments bring satisfaction and contentment in life.

It is just like the nature, which provides us with a subtle companionship, it stays in the background and not too evident in our daily lives sometimes, but it is always present to comfort us, nurture us and inspire us

Perception

Let us face it, you are never going to see God, as like in the vision- which various scriptures provide us with. But yes, you can see his/her glimpses, in the unconditional love, that whoever so offers you in your life- like your mother, father, brother, sister, partner, friend or your pet. By all their actions, they try to show their love to you. Although, they have imperfections like everybody have, and you might not agree with them wholly sometimes. But any act or things said, that are full of love, without the want of anything in return, just to uplift somebody or something is part of the divinity. In these rare glimpses, we can sight the divine love.

And no single person at even given time, can withhold the whole divinity in a single form. As the divine energy or God, as scriptures say, is scattered everywhere, and is in everything. And we all know everything is connected. This same energy itself, gives and gives, without wanting anything in return. Be it the soil- that offers us food, in the form of crops, or deeper layers that offer us fuel wanting nothing- in return. Even though, we have blasted her millions of times and will continue to do so. It will still offer us protection, unconditional love, supports us, in whatever we strive for as always.

Naturally

Everything should come naturally from within, just like- water flowing in a serene calm river, budding sapling growing effortlessly in wild. Similarly, everything mentioned in the book, should occur without any hesitation, and should come naturally from within. This will only happen - when one does not have any guilt from within, and everything that comes along, it does with a strong conviction which is straight from the heart or soul (whatever you want to call it).

Nature has patterns and rhythms everywhere, and in everything - be it in sea waves; in the process of evaporation and condensation; in the weather cycle; in our own breath which is in a rhythm or our heart beats that beats in a pattern. Our emotions and mood also have a pattern, sometimes high /sometimes low. Main thing is that- what goes up or goes high is - bound to get low, energy moves in peaks and troughs. So does an individual's situation or time in life, when you reach peak, stay on it for a while, you will come down. This is bound to happen. As old age sayings also mention this - when you go up the hill, the only way left after that is down. So, what does all this mean, what are we trying to achieve or learn through this?

It means that being in the middle of the wave or taking the middle path is the best place to be in any situation or in the time faced in life. When one does not go high, there is no fear of down, as one will stay in the middle and there will be no down phase. Now what does- staying in middle mean?

It means that you do not go up with emotions, because we all know what entails after that, downward spiral. Do not accept the respect and fame, that comes in your way. Do not become happy with the up phase (a bit difficult to get used to it at first), so that when there comes a time of no recognition or disrespect or lack of respect you do not feel sad. Do this, by staying neutral and expecting nothing from- everything and everyone. All this can be done by staying centered on nothing. Or expanding the self and staying centered on everything, that exists (except for yourself). By becoming the seer or observer of the situations or self, so that we see them, without getting entangled in them, or lusting over them. Saying that this particular thing is happening to - for example, to Kadambari as a person, but my inner soul is untouched by it. As we all know that nothing, can touch or phase that inner source or energy, shared by everybody. And you keep surrendering all your good, and bad emotions to this source.

How will this happen?

If you look closely, with a scientific point of view- a particle goes up and down through the matter. Or the energy travels through the particle, example light or sound waves, travel through particles of the matter, in this fashion. But if you remove particles and create a vacuum. No, up - down of energy waves would happen, through particles or there will be attainment of null, or the null will exist. This null or vacuum is irrespective of time or space. Same way, if we at any given time, consider any given situation in life- we should be in null zone of nothingness (middle stability), which should not lead to the peaks and troughs of emotions. We should have a stable demeanor through it all. This way we will win over peaks and troughs and will gain stability.

Experience everything, in moderation that is the tool - to open all the doors, of anywhere you want to be, or achieve anything in life. Anything of excess is dangerous, as just the rule of energy of equilibrium is trying to achieve every second of life, the energy has to be balanced somehow. What goes up, shall be bought down to stabilize the whole system. So, if you do everything in moderation, meaning you do everything in moderation or stay in the middle zone. Try not to control the cravings of senses, they are natural and innate but if you try to moderate them. Then you will reach this middle zone.

Eat in moderate lengths, sense of smell for example should be like- It is fine, if I smell something bad. It is fine not to feel smooth legs and arms all the time etc. So do every activity, in moderation- without getting entangled in it and you will be free. The light of your inner source will travel through the vacuum, and you will be one with everything. or you will get a glimpse of formless energy.

As this journey, is all about from form to formless. As we know the forms keep changing of energy, but the formless source of energy is the main revering point. Also, in all the scriptures they say, see god everywhere -in all the forms visible and not visible. Similarly, you might recognise one form of revered god or point of love and then spread it everywhere, in everything. You have a wide variety of god forms to choose from or nature itself or parents or near and dear ones, and then you will start recognising the presence of formless element, that exists everywhere, in everything.

Do not wait

For anybody, anything, anytime just start from now!

First of all, please stop waiting, for somebody to come into your life. Who would change it, magically overnight? Nobody has this kind of power except yourself. You yourself, are the key. First, untangle yourself from all the complications, habits, guilt trips, past life and soon you will be free. You will become just like the speck of sand or the mirror, that reflects every ray of sun that comes its way and shines with full glory. Forget that -I will be able to answer all your questions about your life, the complications you have faced or facing now etc. but yes, I can guide you. But this particular common feat, everybody can do, what is special about me? Nothing. Unless you start imbibing the changes in your life. Somebody or else, have been beating this drum from millennia, and will until millennia but it should strike a chord with you. Focus is you, not me, here. The main point is, when do you start or begin to expand (as I would not say change). When do you start this journey? If you really, really want to bring expansion in your life, it will start happening just now. Even this realisation is enough.

The biggest and the simplest change is of - becoming the observer.

So, stop waiting, for someone, magically coming into your life, holding everything that you are seeking in their hands for you. It is simply impossible. Those people who claim to do so, are just thugging you. Because your life is complete and made up of several people, and one person cannot give you each and everything in life, for example- you will still need somebody to be your partner in sharing and caring, parents to love and guide you unconditionally, maybe child love if you want, good friends, good inspiring colleagues. You grab energy from everywhere. Not a single person. One person can guide you from the form- to formless state of energy that prevails everywhere, in everything. But that one person cannot be the key. The key is you, yourself. They can give you theory but practical is to be performed by you.

Chapter 5

TRUTH – THE CONCLUSION

As you have started to open your eyes to yourself. You will slowly but surely realise the truth of your life.

Untainted by the past events, the situations created, you would have the courage to forgive yourself and others and move from your limited self- on to the vast infinity and beyond.

Let us see a checklist, following which- you can tick your way- to your own infinite self!

✓ Not thinking about past events, always being in the present moment.

✓ Release yourself of the guilt of anything or any event, just let it pass. Now your internal eyes are open, you will just seem them as a role this body had to play in any event, this will be achieved without tarnishing the soul within.

✓ Not thinking about yourself all the time or do not indulge in self-pity, replace me with you or us. It is related to your own betterment, your progress and expansion and guess what? It favours everybody around you at this very moment. One plan brings two good things to fruition.

✓ Always either magnify things like theory of relativity or go deep, digging minutely into things, like quantum mechanics. If these paths considered, the behaviour of the concerned particle or body is so complicated and is so mysterious. In this process, of trying to understand which, you will have to- leave all your concerns and live stress free.

For example, if you are worrying and waiting for a result, you have two options, either magnify it, and realise that life is too short to worry about anything in this world. As your form will die one day, be it whatever, you have achieved in this life. And nothing is worth achieving, by taking any amount of stress- because everything is going to nullify one day. Or the other way of looking at the situation is, you can become as negative as you want, saying that -I will fail this result and then what? Ask the question leading to situations then what, then what, then what and it will all lead up to the same consequence- then I will die one day. And then the phrase will convert into so what? So, what if I fail, so what if that happens? it will lead to dying one day. So, all these conclusions will give you so much peace of mind, making you realise that there is absolutely nothing in this world to worry about.

Just like planet keeps revolving round sun but keep on rotating by itself as well, on their own axis. Similarly, situations keep changing in one's life and one's outlook also keeps changing (might feel good about something/somebody good one day, while other day it changes). And, then the outbreak comes in situation or time of the self. And slots into the dawn position of planet and sun, when the darkness dispels, and situation gets resolved on its own. Either through change in time or situation or change in oneself. Just like when the revolving and rotating planet changes position more so and reaches the sun, and sun shines its rays on the revolving planet bringing the dawn or resolution of problem/situation.

✓ Without if and buts, just enjoy the present moment with whatever you have got. You might see and count whatever you possess, as little. As all the humans have a tendency to mull over negative things. But the second you count your blessings; more positivity will follow. Energy is needed to make everything big or small, a zygote to human is formed, when mother feeds in the energy. If we keep feeding negative energy, a big negative will form. While if you feed positive thoughts to yourself, every second of existence you will surely be full of positivity, not only benefitting you, but everybody who is linked to you.

Things that will help you:

1) Surrendering every day to the divine, or that mysterious power in science - that governs everything and everybody. Things seen and unseen by our eyes that governs, or rules - be it gravity, electromagnetic waves, gamma rays, X- rays, microwave waves. Just acknowledging this power. Like rainbow looks beautiful, every single time we see it, and we think it is real, although we all know it is part of an optical illusion. Similarly, we forget, that our bodies function so differently within. Bodies just seem, like a mere form of an object and are so different, to how we feel within ourselves, its similar to just like an illusion. Do you ever realise the moments when oxygen is going up your arteries? Or how the single muscle fibre, twitches to produce the movement of your finger? Can you really comprehend it all, are you aware of it all? No, you do not

give it a second thought you just assume these processes, are happening inside your body. You just assume the connection of your inner voice, that you hear inside your head, to this body. It is surreal. There is so much that science, has not been able to find out about human body, and many functions and processes are still a mystery. There are various events that are happening all the time in anybody's life. One does not know how they come about, who controls them? These are the workings of the energy. But you have you have to raise yourself, out of them. How?

By feeling the energy's presence in every dealing.

Practical (Where and how)

While you are having your shower/bath, surrender whatever you are feeling- to the energy. After all, energy has everything in control.   Be it your bad emotions/experiences of events or anticipation/anxiety of events or situations. Saying "This is all yours- this body/ these paths of life/ these situations that you bring to me or go through along with me. When you start doing it every day, you will see a shift in your consciousness. You will feel less burdened and freer and start recognising observer ship. Why shower time? As everyone takes shower and it is the simplest and economical - timewise if you are pressed for time. When water touches our body, it has a calming/ relaxing affect and is somehow connected to the source within. The first second, that the water touches your body, you feel so relaxed. And with refreshed mind and body you can perform this routine and get connected to your relaxed higher self.

2) Your subtle eyes from within, will guide you and show you, your own journey. They will show you, exactly where you stand, what is contracting your inner self or the bad habits that are, what you need to change for your very own sake. For example, any constrictive behaviour pattern or fear of something.

Law of reaction, states that for every action, there is a reaction. Be it opposite as it is proved, or somewhat similar. I would add, but all I would say is -whatever you do, you make an action of it or people might say karma, out of it. And you would either get an action related to it or reaction related to it. For example, if am sacred of driving, I will not drive which would have further implications in my life or reactions in my life, as result of that particular fear. It will in turn play up, whenever there is a need of driving or mention of driving. So why create unnecessary actions and reactions, which lead to more constrictions, and which further narrows down one's energy. Energy should be expansive, nothing binding or bogging oneself down.

It should be just like, your consciousness feels like- the sky, arms open wide and free to fly anywhere, anyhow with no limit whatsoever.

Practical (How)

You do this by - Challenging yourself and saying to yourself, I want to expand, and I will expand. Nothing or nobody can stop me from being who I can be.

Start doing things you most fear of, face your challenge win over it and expand your consciousness, leave the looming dark cloud of restriction behind you, and become the infinite space.

3) See yourself, in everybody around you. The same energy, you hold within, is in everybody and everything. The same particles make our composition, they act in the same way, and bear the same laws. We are no different to one another. We can understand, sense each other, as we belong to the same energy source. So, as you love yourself, as you forgive yourself so easily, when you do a mistake, same way forgive anybody that hurt you. In the end, you will be at peace by doing this. Simply love everybody, as you love yourself.

How

You do this by- treating everybody as a part of you, if some unpleasant personalities come up, forget, and forgive them for not their sake- but your very own sake. Remember everybody might have different personalities, but we all share the same air, same earth, same universe.

Love everybody as your very own.

By now you should know everything about you, your strengths your weaknesses. Your whole persona and how easily you can step out of it. As you know it, just like one removes one clothes that represents your form. Remove your persona and become nothing or infinite self. In however, way you might choose - occasionally, or constantly and enjoy your connection with yourself and the energy. Along with your very new self-identification.

Thanks for reading this book and all your patience while doing so. Even if you do not do anything, but just start becoming aware of your own self. Your journey has started, or I would say even completed. Because only that is all needed, in every time and in everything.

References

❖ Perkowitz, S. (2018, February 22). E = mc2. Encyclopedia Britannica. https://www.britannica.com/science/E-mc2-equation

❖ Britannica, T. Editors of Encyclopaedia (2017, September 20). Hawking radiation. Encyclopedia Britannica. https://www.britannica.com/science/Hawking-radiation

❖ Britannica, T. Editors of Encyclopaedia (2021, March 10). Stephen Hawking. Encyclopedia Britannica. https://www.britannica.com/biography/Stephen-Hawking

❖ https://www.researchgate.net/publication/323746650_Bohr's_Complementarity_Completed_with_Entanglement

❖ Wikipedia contributors. (2021, February 22). Bell's theorem. In Wikipedia, The Free Encyclopedia. Retrieved 21:45, March 14, 2021, from https://en.wikipedia.org/w/index.php?title=Bell%27s_theorem&oldid=1008322154

❖ Wikipedia contributors. (2021, March 10). Copenhagen interpretation. In Wikipedia, The Free Encyclopedia. Retrieved 21:46, March 14, 2021, from https://en.wikipedia.org/w/index.php?title=Copenhagen_interpretation&oldid=1011382562

❖ Britannica, T. Editors of Encyclopaedia (2020, May 27). Conservation of energy. Encyclopedia Britannica. https://www.britannica.com/science/conservation-of-energy

❖ Wikipedia contributors. (2021, February 23). Second law of thermodynamics. In Wikipedia, The Free Encyclopedia. Retrieved 12:07, March 17, 2021, from https://en.wikipedia.org/w/index.php?title=Second_law_of _thermodynamics&oldid=1008405692

❖ Wikipedia contributors. (2021, March 17). Newton's law of universal gravitation. In Wikipedia, The Free Encyclopedia. Retrieved 12:10, March 17, 2021, from https://en.wikipedia.org/w/index.php?title=Newton%27s_la w_of_universal_gravitation&oldid=1012610898

❖ Wikipedia contributors. (2021, March 10). Copenhagen interpretation. In Wikipedia, The Free Encyclopedia. Retrieved 12:15, March 17, 2021, from https://en.wikipedia.org/w/index.php?title=Copenhagen_int erpretation&oldid=1011382562

❖ Wikipedia contributors. (2021, March 12). Quantum entanglement. In Wikipedia, The Free Encyclopedia. Retrieved 12:21, March 17, 2021, from https://en.wikipedia.org/w/index.php?title=Quantum_entan glement&oldid=1011683908

❖ Wikipedia contributors. (2021, February 25). Quantum biology. In Wikipedia, The Free Encyclopedia. Retrieved 12:22, March 17, 2021, from

https://en.wikipedia.org/w/index.php?title=Quantum_biolo
gy&oldid=1008854093

❖ Wikipedia contributors. (2021, March 10). Theory of
relativity. In Wikipedia, The Free Encyclopedia. Retrieved
12:24, March 17, 2021, from
https://en.wikipedia.org/w/index.php?title=Theory_of_relat
ivity&oldid=1011433200

❖ Wikipedia contributors. (2021, March 8). Spacetime. In
Wikipedia, The Free Encyclopedia. Retrieved 12:30, March
17, 2021, from
https://en.wikipedia.org/w/index.php?title=Spacetime&oldi
d=1011056585

❖ Wikipedia contributors. (2021, February 16). Wave. In
Wikipedia, The Free Encyclopedia. Retrieved 12:35, March
17, 2021, from
https://en.wikipedia.org/w/index.php?title=Wave&oldid=1
007054674

❖ Wikipedia contributors. (2021, March 8). Vacuum. In
Wikipedia, The Free Encyclopedia. Retrieved 12:37, March
17, 2021, from

https://en.wikipedia.org/w/index.php?title=Vacuum&oldid=1010916552

Author's Bio

Kadambari Madhok has been writing since the age of 12. She loves to view everything through the eyes of science- be it spirituality or philosophy. She has undying love for nature which is reflected in all her writings. She has written many poems over the years, which are available through her amazon e book, while in the video format through her you tube channel.

Printed in Great Britain
by Amazon

63395974R00047